nders often try to leave their victims confused. It minimizes their chances of being reported on.
ys and girls: may you never need to use the lessons taught in this book. May your childhood be filled with
ndships, fun and favor. May you come to know how perfectly and wonderfully made you are. If you do ever need
se lessons, know that you deserved better. It was not your fault and you were not responsible to stop it.

ssings
li and Wanda

The Unsafe Neighbour

Written By Dr. Kelli Palfy & Dr. Wanda Polzin

rents and Caregivers How To Use This Book

Give yourself credit for taking healthy steps to inform yourself and your child about sexual abuse and safety. Each of us can make a difference to opening up the conversation and committing to changing stigma around the topic of child sexual abuse.

Familiarize yourself with the enclosed "Information Sheet" and the "Offender's Grooming Techniques" sheet.

Please read this book ahead of reading it WITH your child. Make sure that you are comfortable with it as well as potential questions that may arise. Take time to review the footnotes and take time to view the related pictures; this book was mindfully created to address difficult issues aimed at supporting children to protect themselves when you are not around.

Do take time to discuss other aspects such as Jay feeling uneasy, speaking up, having resources/people to connect with, his ability to pay attention to his 'gut feelings' and/or inner voice.

Remind your child(ren) that they can express and deal with big feelings in various ways such as art, movement, talking, playing, etc.

Ask your child(ren) questions about who is safe to them (and why), what their "Safe Place" is like, etc. All of these types of interaction build attachment and connection!

Have your child role play their knowledge of what they learn including the difference between a secret and a surprise and what to do if someone asks them to keep a secret or touches them.

FORMATION SHEET:

ic Statistics about Child Sexual Abuse:

In Canada, experts estimate as many as 1/6 girls and 1/12 boys experience sexual abuse involving genital contact prior to the age of 18.

When all types of sexual abuse are combined, including other sexual touching and exposure to pornography or sexual material, the number of children sexually abused may be as high as 1/3 girls and 1/6 boys.

THINGS TO KEEP IN MIND AS A CAREGIVER:

- Support YOUR CHILD in learning proper anatomically correct language (not slang) to describe their "private parts".

- Talk with your child about having "no secrets", just surprises. This helps them to recognize that they can speak up about things that are important.

- Talk about and have a predetermined safety plan for if/when they are ever scared or are faced with a concern.

- Allow and respect a child's personal space and ability to say "no". If this is practiced in advance, it can be done assertively (instead of either passively or aggressively). This includes with other family members (i.e., don't force a hug or kiss)

- Talk about consent with your child, letting them know that a child can NEVER consent to inappropriate sexual advances (verbally, physically, or otherwise).

- Teach your child about sexual abuse (and the different types).

Types of Child Sexual Abuse:

(1)   Exposure Abuse

(2)   Non-genital Touching

(3)   Genital Contact

(4)   Penetrative Abuse

(5)   Online/Internet Exposure Abuse

(6)   Production/Distribution Of Child Pornographic Images

Myths About Child Sexual Abuse:

- Sexual Abusers/Offenders are usually strangers. This is a myth. Most sexual offenders are known to a child and to their family.

- Child Sexual Abusers are always adults. This is a myth. Offenders can be other children/teens as well as adults. Sometimes offenders can also be siblings or other children within extended families.

- Children lie about sexual abuse. This is a myth and is very uncommon.

- Sexual abuse can only happen in person. This is a myth. There are online risks which include content risks (exposure to inappropriate and/or unwelcomed words or images), contact risks (participation in risky interactions and communications where a perpetrator may seek contact with a child for a sexual purpose), and conduct risks (where a child contribute knowingly or unknowingly to giving forth sexual images).

- I would know if my child was sexually abused. This is a myth. Many children do not understand that the acts preformed on them as a child are sexual. They often come to realize this only later in life.

Jay (age 7) is the oldest child in his family of 5.
He loves being the big brother to his younger sisters
Erica (who is 5) and Stephanie (who is 9 months). On
cold and rainy days Jay enjoys watching cartoons inside
with Erica.

On sunny days, they both like playing hide and seek or
tag and building tree forts in their yard. Stephanie is
too young to play the same games as Jay and
Erica. She mostly just likes to be cuddled and fed.

Jay's mom is a nurse who works at a long-term care facility. She takes care of elderly patients who need help with things like feeding, bathing and dressing themselves. Although she loves being a mom, she also loves being able to help these people and they really like her. At dinner she often tells funny stories about the elderly folk who like making her laugh.

Jay's dad works at a lumber yard not far from where they live. He's in charge of selling wood to builders and often brings home scraps of wood which they use for building tree forts and family bon-fires.

On school days, Jay and his sister always walk to school together in the mornings. Jay walks home by himself in the afternoon since Jay's mother picks Erica up at lunch time. Erica is in Kindergarten and only goes to school half days for now.

After school, Jay walks home a different, longer way because he likes to walk by Mr. Douglas' house.
Mr. Douglas (who works with Jay's father at the lumber yard), raises puppies, and Jay loves seeing the puppies play in the yard.

Jay is particularly fond of one of the puppies he has nick-named 'Jet', because he is "jet black". Jet always races out to the fence to greet Jay when he walks by. Mr. Douglas has other puppies, but Jet has always been his favorite.

Jet
Joe
Jill

Jay loves Jet so much that he hardly even notices the other puppies, except to take note that Jet is a bit rough with them! Jet is the biggest of all the puppies and he loves to hunt and tackle his siblings, sometimes a little too aggressively!

Jay loves to watch Jet play. Jet seems to admire Jay too; whenever Jay was watching, he shows off his hunting and tackling skills. Being the biggest puppy Jet has a bit of an unfair advantage!

One day, Mr. Douglas was outside giving Jet a bath when Jay walked by. Jet jumped right out of his bath and ran over to say hello to Jay. It was clear he was happy to see Jay since he was wagging his soapy tail. When Jet did this, Jay knew that Jet loved him as much as he loved Jet!

Mr. Douglas was quick to notice how much Jet loved Jay, so he asked Jay if he'd like to come inside the fence and play with him sometime. Jay wanted to go in, but he knew he needed to ask his parents first. They had a rule that any time Jay wanted to go to a friend's house he needed to ask first.

TREATS

At dinnertime Jay asked his father if it was okay for him to go into Mr. Douglas's yard to play with Jet. Since his father knew Mr. Douglas from work, he said yes. Jay made sure he had all of his chores done for the rest of the week so he could start visiting his new friend Jet on a regular basis.

Mr. Douglas seemed to like that Jay was coming to visit. He allowed Jay to brush Jet and asked him to help him bath him. Jet was always rolling in the mud and needed a lot of baths!

Mr. Douglas also had Jay feed Jet and taught Jay how to train him to do tricks like sit, and fetch a ball. Jay was allowed to give Jet treats when he got it right.

Jet

Jay loved teaching Jet and Jet loved spending time with Jay. Jay told his mother how sad he'd be if Mr. Douglas ever sold Jet, and asked if they could buy Jet.

His parents said they couldn't, but told Jay that he could keep helping Mr. Douglas with the new puppies each time they were born. Jay liked this idea, but secretly hoped Jet wouldn't sell. When the time came for the puppies to be sold, Jay grew very sad. Mr. Douglas saw this, and offered to keep Jet as long as Jay agreed to keep working with him, especially when he was away. Jay agreed.

A few weeks later, Mr. Douglas made plans to go to his cabin and offered to pay Jay $10 a day to take care of Jet. It hardly seemed like work at all! Jay liked the idea of having a job, and of making extra spending money!

Jay took good care of Jet. He fed Jet, worked on his training and made sure he got lots of attention. When Mr. Douglas returned he was very pleased with the job Jay had done. He said he might have a few other Jet related chores he could do if he wanted more hours. Mr. Douglas said that he needed help bringing in the big bags of dog food in from the truck and cleaning up doggie do-do from the yard. Soon after, Jay almost regretted having taken the job! It seemed like he was always cleaning up doggie do-do! Jet was getting to be a big dog and he poo-ed a lot! It was a good thing Jay loved Jet, even though he didn't love that chore!

Mr. Douglas was re-finishing his cabin and went away a lot. He often took 2 older boys along with him to help haul lumber and move dirt. Jay was happy to take care of Jet while he was gone and continued to work on his training. Jet was getting really good at tricks now that he was a bit past the puppy stage. Mr. Douglas continued to teach Jay how to train Jet to do more and more advanced skills. He paid Jay by the week and let him come and go as pleased. He even gave him a key to his house for the times when he went away.

DOG

Not losing Mr. Douglas's key felt like a lot of responsibility, one Jay wasn't really comfortable with. He also wasn't comfortable having to carrying the heavy bags of dog food alone. Jay thought of telling Mr. Douglas the bags were too heavy for him, but he didn't want him to know he was struggling to do what he'd promised he would. Jay felt weird about the tickling but he kept silent about that too. Mr. Douglas seemed to know anyways, he would often try to tickle Jay while he was carrying the big heavy bags.

Jay also kept silent about the fact that he found being inside Mr. Douglas' house a little creepy too!
Mr. Douglas often left inappropriate magazines around. Even though Jay never looked at them, he could see, based on their covers, that they had nude pictures in them. Jay knew his parents wouldn't approve of him looking at photos like that.

Months later when Mr. Douglas planned to go to the cabin and the older boys couldn't go, he asked Jay if he wanted to come. Mr. Douglas said he needed help keeping track of Jet since he planned to take him, plus he had other odd jobs like hauling wood and shoveling dirt. He said they would also take time to do a nice hike along the lake and maybe even go fishing. Jay had been working for Mr. Douglas for over a year and liked the idea of spending time at his cabin in the mountains with Jet, so he asked his father. Much to Jay's surprise, his father again said yes!

At the cabin, Mr. Douglas became a little more playful. He started calling Jay "J.J." and told him to call him by his first name. Jay felt uncomfortable and kept calling Mr. Douglas by his full name. Calling him by his first name felt odd. Mr. Douglas had Jay doing jobs like cutting wood and hauling dirt. Jay hadn't ever been allowed to use an axe before and found doing these jobs exciting, but also tiring.

After dinner Mr. Douglas said they would watch a movie together. He let Jay watch a movie he was sure his parent's would not approve of. It contained swear words and naked people in a bedroom scene. He'd never seen a naked woman before and couldn't stop looking at her and watching what they were doing.

Jay felt a bit uncomfortable because he knew his parents wouldn't approve. He decided just to play with Jet and then to fall asleep while Mr. Douglas watched the end of the movie by himself. This was easy since he had made a bed up in front of the TV. Jay slept peacefully and woke up to a beautiful day with a clear view of some mountains. Mr. Douglas was making breakfast. He told Jay it was important that he had a good meal since he planned to take Jay and Jet up a mountain.

The hike was tough, but the view at the top was amazing. Mr. Douglas poked at Jay playfully for being so tired, then tried to give him a hug and told him he had done good. Jay felt weird hugging him.

At dinner, Jay wasn't as hungry as usual. He was tired because he had hiked to the top of a mountain! But when Mr. Douglas suggested they have a relaxing evening and they watch another movie, he felt uncomfortable. He asked Jay if he'd enjoyed the movie they'd watched last evening. Jay didn't know what to say and he began to feel nervous about what type of movie Mr. Douglas planned to watch. He decided not to worry about it since he'd never be able to stay awake to watch a movie anyway.

Jay got inside his sleeping bag. Mr. Douglas encouraged him to sleep naked like the couple in the movie from the night before. He told him he'd sleep better if he did. Jay didn't understand. He slept just fine with his clothes on, and left his pj's on.*

Shortly after Jay fell asleep, he felt Mr. Douglas started to touch his penis. Jay wasn't sure what Mr. Douglas was doing, so he squirmed away from him, but couldn't fall back to sleep. He was too upset. A few hours later Mr. Douglas started touching him again. This time he whispered, "It's ok", "it would feel nice". He touched Jay for a few minutes then rolled over and left Jay alone. Jay was frightened. He knew from a talk he'd had with his parents a few years prior that Mr. Douglas touching him like this was not ok. He knew Mr. Douglas had touched his penis on purpose and it scared him.

* Teaching point - If an adult or older child ever asks you to take your clothes off, say 'no'. It may be difficult to say no to someone older and bigger than you. They may even tell you if you don't obey, you will be in trouble. This isn't true. Say 'no' and tell your parent. You won't be in trouble.

The next day, Mr. Douglas acted as if nothing had happened the night before. Jay was confused and sad but he just decided to act like everything was normal too. He secretly couldn't wait to get home. Although he didn't understand why Mr. Douglas had touched him the way he did, he planned to tell his father about it later.

* Teaching point - Offenders will often act as if everything is normal, especially to the victim's caregiver. If people act one way in front of your parents/caregivers and very differently when you are alone with them, tell your parents.

When Mr. Douglas dropped Jay back off at home, he shook his father's hand and told him what a great help Jay had been. He said he hoped he could hire him to help again.

After he had left, Jay told his father that Mr. Douglas had touched his penis while he was in his sleeping bag. Jay's father was upset. He asked Jay if he was ok, and told him that was Mr. Douglas had done to him was not ok. He also explained that Mr. Douglas could not be trusted so Jay was not to go see him anymore.

Jay was relieved to not see Mr. Douglas anymore, but he was very sad because he also knew that he would likely not be able to see Jet any more either!

Poli

Jay's father made it clear that he wasn't even allowed to walk by the Mr. Douglas' house, not even to see Jet. He made sure Jay understood that he had not done anything wrong, in fact, he had done the right thing when he told his father what Mr. Douglas had done. Adults should never touch children that way.

Jay's father called the police and within a few hours, they came and talked to Jay about what had happened at the cabin.

Jay heard the police man tell his father that this was not the first time Mr. Douglas had done something like this. The police said they had other recent complaints about Mr. Douglas having taken other young boys to his cabin and touching them too! They thanked Jay for telling them and said it would help make sure other kids don't have this happen to them.

For the next two days Jay was very sad. He missed Jet and he missed hanging out at Mr. Douglas' place and doing chores. It had been fun working there. He'd grown to like Mr. Douglas before he touched him at the cabin. Now he didn't. Jay felt tricked and angry at Mr. Douglas.

Jet

Jay's father explained to him that Mr. Douglas was not a healthy man, and that he needed to go away for a special type of treatment. As soon as his father mentioned this, Jay worried about what was going to happen to Jet.

Jay's father told him that Jet had be taken to an animal shelter the day prior, and that he was awaiting adoption to his new forever home. Jay asked his dad if they could adopt Jet? His father said that if Jet was still at the shelter the next day, that they would go get him! All night long, Jay hoped and prayed that Jet would still be there.

Jet

The next day, Jay and his father went to the animal shelter and picked Jet up. Although none of them ever saw Mr. Douglas again, they were all just fine with that. Even Jet seemed fine! He settled into his new forever home with his best friend Jay and his family!

ffender's Grooming Techniques

Those who commit sexual crimes against children often engage in deliberate gestures that are specifically designed to win the trust of their potential victim and their parent.

They situate themselves in the places children attend, become attentive to the child's or parents' needs, are deceivingly transparent about their intentions to assist, and mislead the parent into feeling at ease with them.

They may pay special attention to those they intend to abuse; play with them, help with homework, hire or fake having a common background or interest.

After establishing trust, predators work toward spending time alone with them and toward increasing their acceptance of physical touch; they tickle or wrestle with them, often in front of their parent so it is deemed acceptable.

They often treat their targets as if they are much older than their actual age by introducing them to coarse language, cigarettes, alcohol or pornography, or other adult novelties. These acts help the offender to establish the risk of being reported on since the child is expected to maintain the secret.

Offenders then work toward a situation where the child has to change his clothes, spend the night or both. They may begin the sexual process by inquiring about their present knowledge of sex, offering to teach them and/or introducing them to pornography and/or masturbation.

They may give or leave pornographic magazines lying around.

The nonsexual touch progresses into overt sexual contact, which is the predator's ultimate goal. - When this happens it is confusing. Their offenders were people they trusted prior to their abuse. Offenders work to confuse their victims; they want them to question and/or doubt whether or not they were actually victims.

TOOLS FOR RELAXATION AND REGULATION

Use of 5 Senses: Make adjustments and learn what calms, versus what activates, a child through:

- Using cold packs; heat packs
- Chewing gum, ice, etc.
- Experimenting with sweet versus salty, versus crunchy…
- Wrapping up in a blanket like a sausage
- Using aromatherapy/various scents
- Visualizations/breathing exercises
- Going for a run; swinging in a swing, other…
- Art/drawing/painting/playing music/drumming
- Yoga/movement/dancing/other
- Many, many more…!
- Butterfly Breathing: Sitting on the floor or chair with hands crossed in front of your chest and thumbs connected and gently tapping (left and right alternately) across one's own chest
- 5 Finger Breathing: Using the outline of one hand, follow slowly with your other hand's pointer finger…breathing in as you follow up and breathing gently out as you follow down your finger(s)
- Box Breathing: Creating a large visual box in front of you, breathing in slowly for 4, then holding for a count of 4, then breathing out for a count of 4, then holding for a count of 4 (4 times)!
- Lazy 8 Breathing: Imagining a large figure 8 on its side in front of you…tracing it with your finger outstretched in front of you, and breathing in for one tracing and breathing out for another tracing (do this as many times as you'd like)
- Cupcake/Candle Breathing: Imagine you have a birthday cupcake (you most favorite) in one hand and a beautiful sparkly candle in the other…. breath in slowly to smell the cupcake and then gently blow out the birthday sparkler/candle that's in your other hand. Repeat as many times as you'd like

Safe Place Exercise (Read aloud and discuss with your child, sharing YOUR place too):

Imagine the most beautiful amazing place you can, knowing that within each one of us we have a "Safe Place". I don't know if your place is real, imaginary… something you've seen in a movie, or a place you've been before…it's your place in your mind….so safe and wonderful. Imagine all the colors in your safe place. notice what's above you, beside you, below you, and behind you…feeling so positive and happy in this place. Pay attention to the temperature of your safe place. is it warm or cool?... Also notice how it feels inside your body…safe, calm, happy. Now, notice if there are any sounds, music or nature sounds perhaps, or maybe it's quite?...Notice if there are any scents or fragrances?..your favorite foods…? Allow yourself a few moments to really be there…there in your safe, magical, wonderful place. And, each and every time that you wish to experience your safe place, you know you can always return to it…

54321 - Pick out 5 things in the room you can see, then 4 things you can reach out and touch, 3 things you can hear, 2 things you can smell or taste and 1 part of your body you are especially aware of.

Source: Check out Little Warriors.ca for available treatment programs for child sexual abuse victims.